Who Needs a JUNGLE?

A Rainforest Ecosystem

KAREN PATKAU

TUNDRA BOOKS

Published in Canada by Tundra Books,
75 Sherbourne Street, Toronto, Ontario M5A 2P9

Published in the United States by Tundra Books of Northern New York,
P.O. Box 1030, Plattsburgh, New York 12901

Library of Congress Control Number: 2011923282

Library and Archives Canada Cataloguing in Publication

Patkau, Karen
    Who needs a jungle? : a rainforest ecosystem / by Karen Patkau.

(Ecosystem series)
ISBN 978-0-88776-992-4

    1. Jungle ecology – Central America – Juvenile literature. 2. Rain forest
ecology – Central America – Juvenile literature. 3. Jungles – Central America –
Juvenile literature. 4. Rain forests – Central America – Juvenile literature. I. Title. II.
Series: Ecosystem series

QH108.A1P38 2012   j577.34'09728   C2011-901374-6

We acknowledge the financial support of the Government of Canada through
the Book Publishing Industry Development Program (BPIDP) and that of the
Government of Ontario through the Ontario Media Development Corporation's
Ontario Book Initiative. We further acknowledge the support of the Canada
Council for the Arts and the Ontario Arts Council for our publishing program.

Medium: Digital

Design: Karen Patkau
Typesetting: Leah Springate

Printed and bound in China

1 2 3 4 5 6   17 16 15 14 13 12

To Dr. Jane Berg,

with special thanks to my family and friends.

WELCOME TO THE JUNGLE

Eyes blink in the dark. A kinkajou peers between rubber tree leaves.

Click-click-click. Snap. SQUAWK! SQUAWK! Hissssss. Grrrrrr. Sounds echo through the warm, sticky air.

Swooping between tree trunks and twisting vines, a little brown bat ambushes flying insects. A margay stalks a sleeping scarlet macaw.

Termites stream across the damp earth and disappear into a hole. They carry bits of dead leaves back to their underground nest for dinner.

It is nighttime in the jungle.

THE JUNGLE IS A RAINFOREST

Around the middle of the earth is an imaginary circle called the equator. There is more sunshine, heat, and rainfall here than any other place in the world.

Lands surrounding the equator are covered in tropical rainforests. There are more kinds of plants and animals here than anywhere else.

Crowded with trees and tangled plants,
the jungle is a rainforest.

LIVING IN THE JUNGLE

Each living thing in the jungle has a purpose that connects it to those around it. The jungle is an ecosystem.

It grows in layers that include the emergent trees, the canopy, the understory, and the forest floor. Different plants and animals live in each layer.

Let's meet more of this jungle's inhabitants.

JUNGLE LAYERS

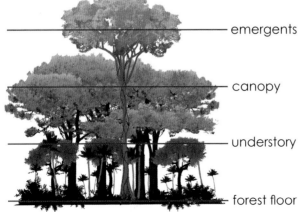

— emergents

— canopy

— understory

— forest floor

Over the canopy, the sky is clear. The air is fresh. A few trees rise above the others. They are called the emergents. Hear the wind rustle through their leaves.

Harpy eagles sit in their nest, high in an emergent kapok tree. Father dives down through the canopy branches. It is his turn to hunt for food.

In the canopy, the air is muggy and still. The branches are filled with life. Vines and tree-dwelling plants thrive in the treetops.

The toucan, howler monkey, red-eyed tree frog, vine snake, and collared anteater are just a few of the animals living here. With plenty of flowers, fruit, seeds, leaves … or creatures to eat, many residents never leave.

After a rainstorm, water drips from the tips of waxy leaves. A two-toed sloth hangs by hooked claws from a moss-covered branch.

A Blue Morpho butterfly flutters about. Parrots glide beneath the treetops.

Orchids, strangler figs, and bromeliads grow on top of other plants. They absorb moisture from the humid air and rain. These plants are epiphytes.

Smaller trees live in the jungle understory. Palms are found here in the canopy's shade.

Lianas are climbing plants that sprout from the earth. They coil their woody vines around young trees, which support the lianas as they grow upward.

Sunlight beams through a space in the canopy leaves, where an old mahogany tree has crashed to the ground. A sapling shoots up to take its place.

Huge Hercules beetles battle on the forest floor.

Spots and stripes camouflage a baby tapir, lying still among the tree roots. He will not become a jaguar's snack!

THE FOOD CHAIN

All living things need food for energy and to survive. They take nourishment from their surroundings. In turn, they nourish others. All are part of a food chain.

Plants make their own food, using the sun's energy, carbon dioxide from the air, and water.

A herbivore is an animal that eats plants. An agouti eats nuts and fruit. A coatimundi eats fruit, small animals, and insects. It is an omnivore.

A boa constrictor eats animals. It is a carnivore.

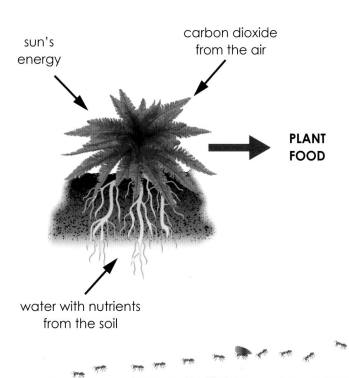

sun's energy

carbon dioxide from the air

PLANT FOOD

water with nutrients from the soil

BACTERIA

LIFE IS A CYCLE

All living things die someday. Their remains are never wasted in the jungle. Scavengers eat dead plants and animals. A turkey vulture eats rotting meat.

Fungi and bacteria live on dead matter, breaking it down into nutrients that are released back into the environment.

Unlike other places, most dead things in the jungle do not fall to the ground and decompose in soil. Because of this, jungle earth is not very fertile.

When plants and animals that live in the treetops die, their decaying matter gathers on branches. It supplies tree-dwelling plants and some insects and animals with nutrients.

JUNGLE TREES PROTECT THE LAND

The rainforest is disappearing. Loggers cut down trees. Workers clear land for farms and cattle ranches, even though the soil is poor for pastures or crops.

Tree and plant roots cling to fine jungle topsoil. Without them, rain washes topsoil away into nearby streams and rivers. The uncovered soil below then dries out and

hardens. It becomes even less nourishing. Topsoil particles then settle to the bottom. If this "silt" builds up, water can overflow and flood land. Silt can also pollute drinking water, clog irrigation systems, and endanger living things that depend on streams and rivers.

THE JUNGLE AFFECTS WEATHER

The leafy treetops of the jungle canopy look like a gigantic bumpy broccoli. Above their uneven surface, air currents become gusty winds.

Wind increases the amount of rainwater that evaporates into the air.

Water vapor gathers, clouds form, and rainfall begins.

Without the jungle, less rain falls. Any rainwater quickly drains from the surface of the dry earth.

When less and less rainfall is recycled, a drought can happen. Then water supplies dry up, and plants cannot grow.

THE AIR AROUND US

The earth's atmosphere is made up of different gases – mostly nitrogen and oxygen. There are small amounts of other gases, too, such as carbon dioxide.

Carbon dioxide is one of the "greenhouse gases" responsible for "global warming." Without jungle plants, the earth's air temperature would rise even higher.

Plants use carbon dioxide to make food. They release oxygen back into the air. Oxygen is necessary for animals, including humans, to breathe.

OXYGEN CYCLE

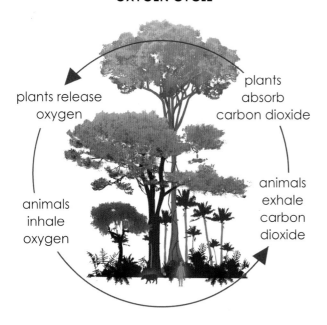

plants release oxygen

plants absorb carbon dioxide

animals inhale oxygen

animals exhale carbon dioxide

WHO NEEDS A JUNGLE?

A jungle is full of treasures. We are still discovering its plants and animals. It supplies us with oxygen, food, medicinal ingredients, and raw materials that we use every day.

Native people have relied on the healing effects of its plants for centuries. Today, modern scientists are learning about them, too. Even snake venom is used in medicine to treat high blood pressure.

Bananas, pineapples, oranges, sweet potatoes, nuts, cocoa, coffee, and sugar first came from the jungle.

Hardwood for furniture, latex in rubber, and plant oil in soap are jungle products.

When the rainforest is destroyed, the homes of plants and animals vanish. Without a place to live, it is difficult for them to survive.

Who needs a jungle? We all do.

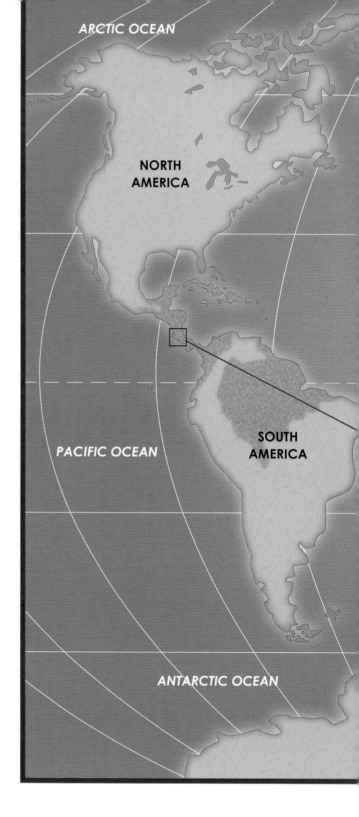

TROPICAL RAINFOREST AREAS OF THE WORLD

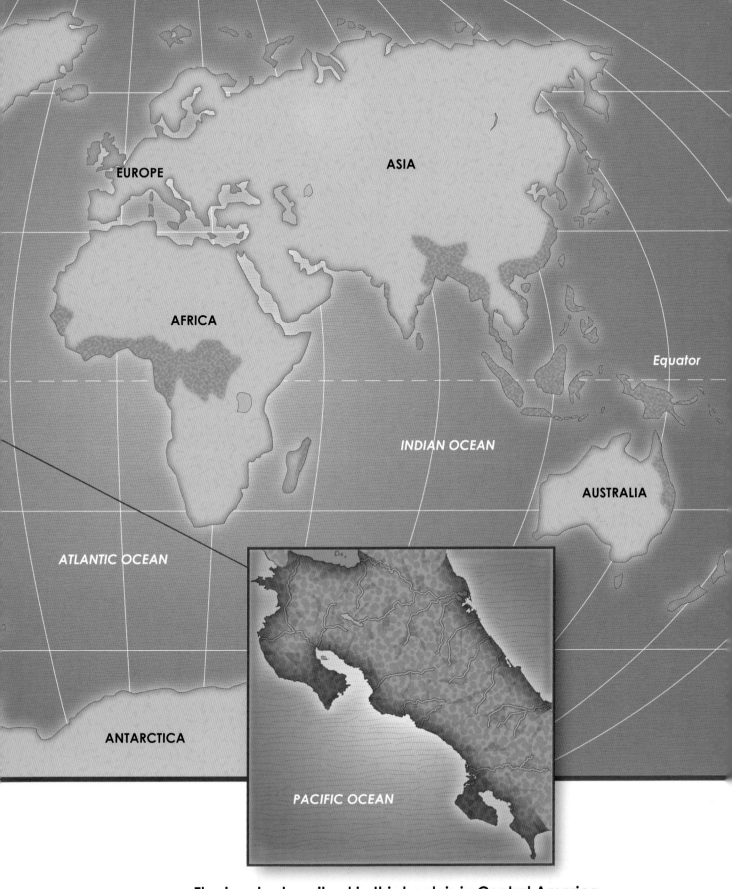

The jungle described in this book is in Central America.

HERE IS MORE INFORMATION ABOUT SOME OF THE JUNGLE INHABITANTS:

Agouti
The shy graceful agouti is a rodent about the size of a rabbit. It is a fast runner and a good swimmer. It cracks open nuts with its strong, sharp teeth.

Blue Morpho Butterfly
Its beating wings flash blue and brown as the Blue Morpho butterfly flutters about the trees. It does not drink nectar, but feeds on rotting fruit and sap.

Boa Constrictor
This big snake grasps its prey with large curved teeth. It tightens its coils around its victim until it suffocates. Then the boa swallows the whole thing.

Bromeliad
Sturdy leaves surround the bromeliad plant's flowering stalk. They overlap tightly at the base and collect rainwater. Insects can be found swimming in little bromeliad pools.

Coatimundi
Awake during the day, the coatimundi sleeps up in a tree at night. It grooms itself and other members of its band with its strong claws and teeth.

Harpy Eagle
The harpy eagle is the biggest and most powerful bird of prey in the jungle. A harpy couple raises one chick every two or three years.

Hercules Beetles

These beetles are called Hercules because they are incredibly strong for their size. Males have very long horns, which they use for fighting other males.

Howler Monkey

The howler monkey is one of the loudest animals in the jungle. Troops of these large monkeys howl fiercely to defend their canopy territory from other troops.

Jaguar

The largest wildcat in Central America is a lonely hunter. It prowls the jungle floor, looking for something to catch and eat. The jaguar likes to swim.

Kapok Tree

The giant kapok grows quickly and towers over other canopy trees. Strong roots emerge from the sides of its trunk and grow down into the ground to support it.

Kinkajou

At night, the kinkajou feeds on fruit and insects. Traveling quickly among treetops, it hangs on to branches and balances with the help of its long tail.

Little Brown Bat

The bat finds flying insects in the dark by sending high-pitched squeaks into the air. The sounds hit an insect and echo back to the bat, telling it where the insect is.

Mahogany Tree
Wide and tall, the mahogany tree is valued for its rich reddish brown wood, used in making fine furniture. Mahoganies are found few and far between in the jungle.

Margay
This small spotted wildcat is about the size of a large house cat. An excellent climber, the margay hunts small animals and birds up among tree branches.

Orchid
Growing high in the canopy, the orchid's dangling roots absorb moisture and dissolved nutrients from the air. Water is stored in "false bulbs," or swollen parts of its stem.

Palm Trees
Palm trees are part of the palm family of plants. Most palms have a branchless trunk, with a crown of fan-shaped leaves. Their leaves stay green year-round.

Red-Eyed Tree Frog
Hiding its bright markings, the red-eyed tree frog sleeps under a leaf by day. When startled, it flashes its big red eyes and leaps away on huge orange feet.

Scarlet Macaw
The magnificent parrot has a loud squawking cry. It likes to eat fruit, nuts, and seeds. A strong and swift flyer, it soars above the canopy with its mate.

Strangler Fig

Dropped into a treetop by a bird, the strangler fig seed sprouts up toward the sun. Its roots wrap tightly around the tree and grow down to the ground.

Tapir

The tapir is a large herbivore. It grasps foliage with its long flexible snout. A young tapir's camouflage spots and stripes disappear as it gets older.

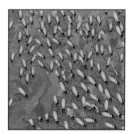

Termites

Termites live in large colonies with many others. They feed mainly on dead plant matter and are destructive to trees. Anteaters, birds, and other creatures eat termites.

Toucan

The toucan is known for its huge multicolored beak, which can grow longer than the bird's body. The beak is lightweight and useful for picking fruit.

Two-Toed Sloth

The slow-moving sloth spends most of its life hanging from tree branches, eating fruit and leaves. Its fur grows downward so that rainwater drains off easily.

Vine Snake

When draped around a branch, the long and pencil-thin vine snake is hard to see. It has a venomous bite, which is not deadly to humans.

GLOSSARY

bacteria – tiny single-celled organisms that break down the remains of other living things

camouflage – to disguise something so that it appears as part of its surroundings

currents – areas of water or air flowing in a certain direction

drought – a long period of time without any rain

ecosystem – a community of plants, animals, and organisms that interact with each other and their physical environment. There are many different ecosystems on Earth.

environment – the surroundings and conditions in which something exists or lives

evaporates – changes from a liquid into a gas or vapor

fertile – capable of producing and nourishing many plants or crops

fungi – nongreen plants, such as mushrooms and molds, which live off other things

global warming – the rise in average temperature of air near the earth's surface since the mid-twentieth century

greenhouse gases – gases in the earth's atmosphere that trap heat. The main greenhouse gases are carbon dioxide, methane, and nitrous oxide.

inhabitants – living things that dwell in a certain place for a period of time

irrigation systems – man-made methods for watering

nourish – to provide a living thing with food or other substances it needs to survive

nutrients – substances that give nourishment to a living thing

prey – an animal that is hunted by another animal for food

sapling – a young slender tree

scavengers – animals that feed on leftover food or plant and animal remains

topsoil – the upper layer of soil that supplies plants with nourishment

tropical rainforest – a dense tropical forest with heavy rainfall

water vapor – tiny water droplets floating in the air

venom – the toxic fluid secreted by animals such as poisonous snakes

venomous – poisonous